Teeny Totty™
Uses Mama's BIG Potty
TRANSITION from Potty Chair to Toilet

story & illustrations by Yvonne Jones

LoewenHerz-Creative

LoewenHerz-Creative

A LOEWENHERZ-CREATIVE BOOK

Published by LoewenHerz-Creative 2013

Teeny Totty™ Uses Mama's Big Potty
Text Copyright © 2013 Yvonne Jones
Illustrations Copyright © 2013 Yvonne Jones

Printed in the USA.

All inquiries should be sent to
info@LoewenHerz-Creative.com

www.LoewenHerz-Creative.com

ISBN-13: 978-0-61586-013-8
ISBN-10: 0-61586-013-3

To my own little Chibi

Wakey, wakey, sleepy head.
Time for Totty to get out of bed.

Brush your teeth,
   your hair straight...

...sit on the potty,
- but uh-oh, wait!

Today is the PERFECT day to learn something new.
Something, that only BIG kids can do.

Potty chair, bye-bye. No more potty.
Only BIG grown-up toilets for BIG Teeny Totty.

"TOILET POWER" is what we'll gain today.
So let's get started! What do you say?

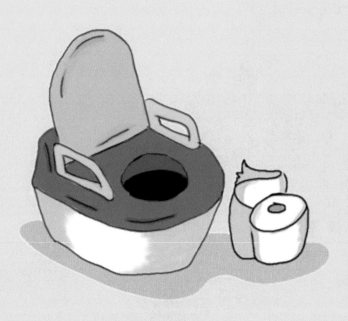

Look, right here - the BIG potty.
Mama uses it EVERY day!

It takes some practice to get used to it.
Now it's Totty's turn - HOORAY!

Big large seat, way up high.
Can't climb up. Why, oh why?!

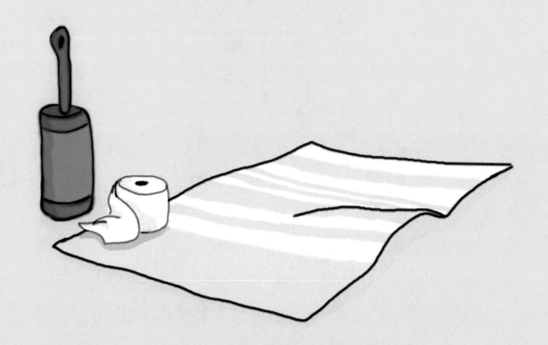

Worried about slipping,
    loud noises, and height.
But Mama's RIGHT here.
    It will ALL be all right.

Here's what we're going to do:
The stepping stool will help us through.

Some boys and girls use a training seat.
You should give it a try if you feel the need.

Whatever you use, it's ALL up to YOU.
As long as you give it a chance and try something new.

Totty decides to give it a try
and uses the stepping stool to get up high.

Up, up, up he goes.

Hands hold on tight, stool touching the toes.

Reading a book. Sitting up high.
Using the toilet. What a brave guy!

Not so different from a potty chair at all.
Sitting up here makes Totty
feel BIG and TALL.

Finally done. Feeling so new.
Using the toilet, just like grown-ups do!

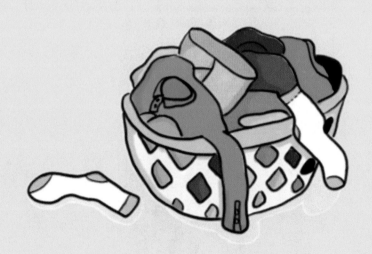

Flushing together. Round and round.
The water makes a gushing sound.

Down flushes the water,
through pipes and a drain.
To a place where it gets cleaned,
so that soon we can use it all over again.

All that is left for Totty to do,
is wash his hands with soap,
and then dry them off, too.

"TOILET POWER" is what you've gained today.
Now give yourself a big HIP HIP HOORAY!

Teeny Totty, oh so proud!
Big hug from Mama. Praises SO loud.

Using the bathroom, just like big kids do.
From potty to toilet. And so can YOU!

Tips for successful transitioning

- Don't rush! Your child already took a very big step by becoming potty trained. Some simply have a harder time than others transitioning from their potty to the grown-up toilet.

- Get ready by telling your child that it is time to use the grown-up toilet, just like Mommy/Daddy/brother(s)/sister(s). Help him/her understand that moving to the grown-up potty is the next step to becoming a big boy/girl.

- Let your child know that the potty will soon be too small for him/her to use, and that this necessitates the transition.

- Help him/her understand that by moving to the grown-up toilet, using the bathroom will be a lot easier when away from home.

- Start by moving your child's potty next to the grown-up toilet and by letting him/her see you use the grown-up toilet.

- Let your child get used to the flushing sound and mechanism by letting him/her flush the toilet whenever you have used to.

- Explain to your child where the waste is flushed to after it leaves the toilet bowl.

- Be patient.

- Praise your child for trying, as well as for succeeding. Never scold or punish.

- Make your expectations clear: You are confident that your child will make the transition.

Be proud of your little one.

Love,

13410979R00029